MY FIRST BOOK OF
RELATIVITY

Button
BOOKS

SHEDDAD KAID–SALAH FERRÓN
& EDUARD ALTARRIBA

CONTENTS

ALBERT EINSTEIN

INTRODUCTION

Albert Einstein's Relativity is the theory of space and time. We all instinctively know what **TIME** and **SPACE** are. Although they seem to be simple concepts, we'll see that if we think about them a bit, fascinating things happen.

When he was a teenager, Einstein used to wonder why something that other people understood perfectly kept on going round and round in his head. Because he questioned it and thought about it so much, many years later he was able to develop his Space-Time theory, the theory of **SPECIAL RELATIVITY**. (It is called this because years later he also developed the theory of **GENERAL RELATIVITY**, which involves space and time as well as other factors like gravity.)

So to understand the Space-Time theory, first we need to understand what each of these two concepts, space and time, really means. And it will also help us to know what movement is and what happens with the speed of light. Then, like Einstein, once we understand these things, we'll be able to understand the world through **RELATIVITY**. And we'll discover that things that seem to be science fiction really do happen in our universe.

Welcome to this amazing journey!

TIME

Someone wakes you up and says that the alarm went off ages ago and you'll have to eat your breakfast quickly if you don't want to be late for school. You stayed up reading late last night and now you wish you hadn't.

You force your eyes open and look at the clock. It's true. You've only got twenty minutes before the bus comes. And you've already been late once this week.

We all know what time is. We use it constantly to know what to do and when to do it. We organize our lives around units of time: seconds, minutes, hours, days, weeks, months, years, etc.

But if someone asks us what time actually is, things get a bit complicated. Great thinkers have tried to define it, but for us the most important thing about time is that we can measure it.

So, how do we measure time?

Einstein was quite clear: **"TIME IS WHAT WE MEASURE WITH A CLOCK."** But how does a clock measure time?

To measure time
we need something to
happen again and again
repeatedly or, to put
it another way,
periodically.

MEASURING TIME

One of the first ways that our ancestors measured time was by using days. A DAY is the time that passes between two consecutive sunrises. Since the Sun rises every day (it is something that happens periodically) it is perfect for measuring time. So, if we count how many times the Sun has risen, we can find out how many days have gone by.

Now we know that the Earth rotates around itself so that, in fact, a day is the time that it takes for the Earth to revolve once around its axis.

Some cultures also measure time by using the phases of the Moon.

Soon people realized that it was not only days that occurred repeatedly but also other phenomena like phases of the Moon every month or seasons every year.

8

MEASURING TIME PERIODS SHORTER THAN A DAY

● *To measure shorter amounts of time we use HOURS, MINUTES, and SECONDS.*

● If we divide the time that a day lasts into 24 equal parts we have an HOUR.

● Then, dividing an hour into 60 equal parts gives us a MINUTE.

● Finally, dividing a minute into 60 equal parts gives us a SECOND.

365 DAYS

24 HOURS

60 MINUTES

60 SECONDS

MEASURING TIME PERIODS LONGER THAN A DAY

● To measure longer amounts of time we use another periodic movement, the Earth moving around the Sun. This is what we call a YEAR.

● A YEAR is the time that the Earth takes to revolve once around the Sun: 365 days. Well, in fact it takes slightly longer, 365.24219 days to be precise. As there is a quarter of a day extra every year, we have added an extra day to the calendar every four years (February 29). That is why LEAP years have 366 days.

● We use this unit of time to say that we are ten years old, that the Great Pyramid of Giza was built about 4,600 years ago, or that the UNIVERSE is about 14 billion years old.

The SECOND is the unit of time most used by scientists.

CLOCKS & WATCHES

Clocks and watches are technological objects that repeat cycles one way or another, enabling us to measure time.

SUNDIALS

These are clocks that have been used since ancient times. They use the shadow of a stick over a marked-out area to find out the position of the Sun and therefore what time of day it is. They are not very accurate, which is why we hardly ever use them these days.

HOURGLASSES

If we turn an hourglass upside down every time the last grain of sand falls through, we have something that happens periodically. If we count how many times we've turned it, we can find out how much time has passed. These days, they are hardly ever used, but for a very long time they were the best way to measure time.

SAILORS USED TO HANG HOURGLASSES, OR SAND CLOCKS, IN THEIR SHIPS. THIS ENSURED THAT THEY ALWAYS STAYED IN A VERTICAL POSITION EVEN WHEN THE SEA WAS ROUGH.

MECHANICAL CLOCKS

These have a mechanism that turns the clock hands. Some move by using weights and others use a coiled spring. The first mechanical clocks were not very accurate and they needed to be wound up regularly. Nowadays, there are more accurate clocks that work with batteries.

THE PENDULUM

Around 1602, Galileo Galilei realized that the side-to-side movement (oscillation) of a pendulum was periodic and could be used to measure time. If we count the number of times that a pendulum swings, we can find out how much time has passed. Pendulum clocks were the first clocks to tell the time accurately.

GALILEO GALILEI

DIGITAL WATCHES

Inside today's wristwatches we find something similar to a tiny pendulum that oscillates. Digital wristwatches have an **ELECTRONIC CIRCUIT** (like a pendulum) which also has oscillations that enable us to measure time.

ATOMIC CLOCKS

Atomic clocks are the most accurate clocks in existence. They are used, for example, to measure time in satellites, laboratories and communications networks. They are based on atomic vibration. They work through the repetitive oscillation of atoms. If we count the oscillations like we do with a pendulum, we can measure time. Today's atomic clocks are so accurate that they will only lose one second in 15 billion years (that's older than the Universe).

11

SPACE

Like we saw with **TIME**, defining **SPACE** can be a bit complicated. We can describe it as the place where objects meet and where things happen. We could call it the stage where reality happens.

So, how do we measure space?

In fact, what we measure is **DISTANCE**, which is the length between two objects. To measure distances we use something **RIGID** and of a fixed length, such as a **MEASURING STICK**.

If we want to know the length between two points, we lay our measuring stick down from one place to another as many times as necessary.

So by counting how many times we've had to lay our stick down, we can find out the distance: two sticks, four sticks, five and a half sticks, etc.

POINT **A**

POINT **B**

But, I hear you say, how long do we make our **MEASURING STICKS**?

Imagine that two building contractors have to build a bridge over a river.

The plans say that the structure will be five sticks high. Each builder starts from a different riverbank and each uses his own stick, which is different from the other builder's stick.

What could go wrong?

In order to avoid problems like these we need to use a **UNIVERSAL MEASUREMENT SYSTEM**.

Some people decided to make a rod of a specific size that we call a **METER**. Ever since then measuring sticks have been made the same size as this rod: one meter long.

This meant that building contractors and everyone else would never again have problems agreeing with one another when it comes to measuring distances.

The meter is the unit of length most used by scientists.

Despite this agreement, some countries also use other units of measurement like the imperial system, where measurement is based on inches, feet, yards, and miles.

MINOR MISHAPS IN SPACE

In 1999, the Mars Climate Orbiter probe crashed into Mars. The probe had been built to fly using the **IMPERIAL SYSTEM OF UNITS** but, before takeoff, it had been given flight instructions using the **METRIC SYSTEM**. Instead of continuing to orbit, it got too close to the planet and disintegrated in Mars's atmosphere.

The length of a **METER** was first established in 1799, when a team of scientists gave the French state a platinum bar as a model for measuring length.

In order to calculate how long this model bar should be, they had to measure the length of the meridian line from Dunkirk to Montjuic Castle in Barcelona. The Spanish and French were at war at the time, but the mission was so important that a French scientific expedition was allowed to travel to Barcelona to do the measurements and the calculations.

DUNKIRK

BARCELONA

Now that we know how to measure time and space, we can work out how fast an object is traveling. In other words, we can work out its

SPEED

The speed of an object is the distance that the object has traveled divided by the time taken to travel that distance.

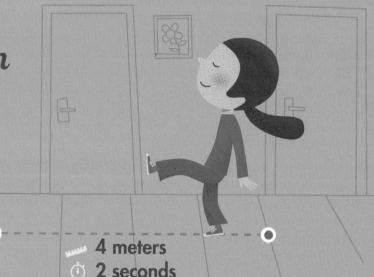

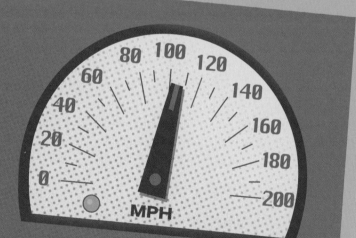

I'm sure that you've seen a speedometer in a car before. It's an instrument that tells you how fast the car is going.

4 meters
2 seconds

Imagine that it takes us 2 seconds to cover a distance of 4 meters. Our speed would be 4 meters every 2 seconds or 2 meters per second, which is the same thing. This is how we write it:

$$v = 2 \text{ m/s}$$

V stands for velocity, another word for speed. You'll see that whenever we want to find out the speed, we divide the distance traveled by the time taken to travel it:

$$\text{Speed} = \frac{\text{distance}}{\text{time}}$$

Doing a hundred!

If a car is traveling at 100 miles an hour (100 mph), that means it will take exactly 1 hour to cover the 100 miles between Town A and City B.

And if it continues at the same speed, it will take 2 hours to cover the 200 miles between City B and Village C.

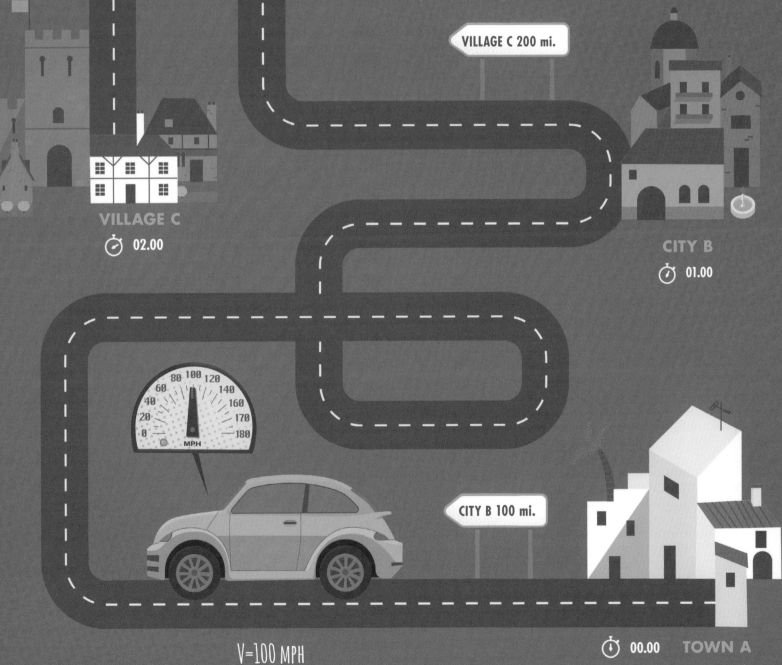

VILLAGE C 200 mi.

VILLAGE C

⏱ 02.00

CITY B

⏱ 01.00

CITY B 100 mi.

V=100 MPH

⏱ 00.00   TOWN A

15

MOVEMENT

An object is MOVING when there is speed. We say that it is AT REST when it is STATIONARY, or at zero velocity, which is the same thing.

DR. ALBERT

ALICE

We're going to do a little thought experiment. Imagine a train that is going past a station without stopping at a constant speed of 30 mph.

Alice is sitting in the train reading a book. For her THE BOOK IS STATIONARY and is not moving, which is why she can comfortably read. In fact, for Alice, EVERYTHING INSIDE THE TRAIN CAR IS AT REST (people, seats, and lights).

If Dr. Albert watches the same train going past from the station platform, for him the scenario would be different. WHAT HE SEES IS THE TRAIN AND EVERYTHING INSIDE IT GOING AT A SPEED OF 30 MPH, and nothing is at rest including people, seats, Alice, and her book.

Einstein spent a lot of time doing thought experiments. He really enjoyed them!

The things that are stationary for Alice are moving for Dr. Albert.

Movement is always defined as relative to something. This is what we call FRAMES OF REFERENCE. →

FRAMES OF REFERENCE

Frames of reference are used to measure positions, distances, and speeds.

We can use two frames of reference to find out the speed of the objects in the train:

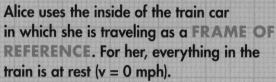

Alice uses the inside of the train car in which she is traveling as a FRAME OF REFERENCE. For her, everything in the train is at rest (v = 0 mph).

THE SPEEDS MEASURED BY ALICE AND BY DR. ALBERT ARE DIFFERENT.

This is why we say that MOVEMENT is RELATIVE and depends on the OBSERVER (the person watching) or the FRAME OF REFERENCE (where they are watching from).

For Dr. Albert, the FRAME OF REFERENCE is the STATION PLATFORM. For him, everything inside the train is traveling at a constant speed (v = 30 mph).

AN INERTIAL FRAME OF REFERENCE IS ONE WHERE THE SPEED IS CONSTANT ALL THE TIME.

Imagine that, for some reason, someone
is lost in his spacesuit in outer space.
There is absolutely nothing there. He
can't see any stars, or his spaceship,
or the Earth. How can he find out his
position if there are no objects? How
can he tell if he's moving or not? And
if he's moving, what is his speed?

Luckily, he wasn't really lost. It turns out that his visor had steamed up and he couldn't see anything. Now he can see the stars, the space station, and the Earth. By looking at these objects, he has a frame of reference, can find out his position, and know that he is moving around the Earth at a speed of about 18,500 miles per hour.

ADDING UP SPEEDS

Now we know what **FRAMES OF REFERENCE** are, we're going to imagine that Alice is still traveling in a train and she starts playing with her remote control car. She makes it go in the same direction as the train.

What speed is the car doing?

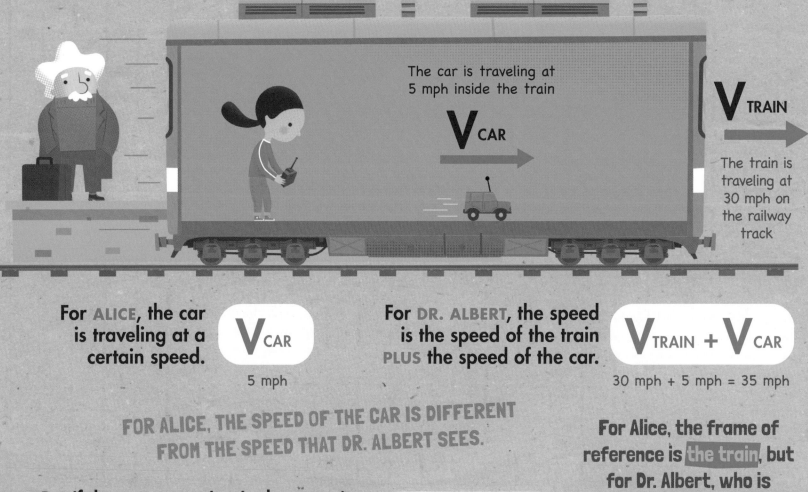

The car is traveling at 5 mph inside the train

$$V_{CAR}$$

$$V_{TRAIN}$$

The train is traveling at 30 mph on the railway track

For **ALICE**, the car is traveling at a certain speed.

$$V_{CAR}$$

5 mph

For **DR. ALBERT**, the speed is the speed of the train **PLUS** the speed of the car.

$$V_{TRAIN} + V_{CAR}$$

30 mph + 5 mph = 35 mph

FOR ALICE, THE SPEED OF THE CAR IS DIFFERENT FROM THE SPEED THAT DR. ALBERT SEES.

But if the car was going in the opposite direction to the train, Dr. Albert would see the speed as the speed of the train **MINUS** the speed of the car.

$$V_{TRAIN} - V_{CAR}$$

30 mph - 5 mph = 25 mph

For Alice, the frame of reference is **the train**, but for Dr. Albert, who is looking at it from outside, the frame of reference is **the platform**.

The same thing happens in any sum involving speed:

A SNAIL ON A TORTOISE

$$V_{SNAIL} + V_{TORTOISE}$$

A CYCLIST ON AN AIRPLANE

$$V_{AIRPLANE} + V_{CYCLIST}$$

AN ARROW FIRED FROM A CAR

$$V_{CAR} + V_{ARROW}$$

It was Galileo Galilei, about 400 years ago, who realized that movement is **RELATIVE** to the frame of reference and that we have to add up the different speeds as we have just explained to work out the movement of an object.

THE SPEED OF LIGHT

One of the fundamental laws of the Universe is that light travels at a constant speed of

300,000 kilometers per second.

And NOTHING can go faster than the speed of light.

LIGHT YEARS

The Universe as we know it is so huge that we calculate distances using a unit of measurement that we call a LIGHT YEAR.

A light year is the distance that light covers during one Earth year, traveling at 300,000 kilometers per second. Try to imagine such an incredible distance!

The nearest stars to us are more than four light years away, and the farthest ones that we know are billions of light years away.

Light travels so fast that in our world it appears instantaneous, but with cosmic distances, it is another story.

For example, the Sun's light takes about 8 minutes to travel the almost 150 million kilometers between the Earth and the Sun.

That means that whenever we look at the Sun, we are looking at it as if it were 8 minutes ago.

If it explodes one day, it will take us 8 minutes to realize!

We always see the past

However fast **LIGHT** goes, it always takes some time to travel from one place to another and we don't see things until their light reaches us.

If some extraterrestrials looked at us now from a planet **4,500 LIGHT YEARS** away, what would they see?

They wouldn't see the Earth as it is now but they would see it as it was **4,500 YEARS AGO**. They would be able to see, for example, how the ancient Egyptians built the pyramids.

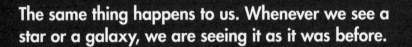

The same thing happens to us. Whenever we see a star or a galaxy, we are seeing it as it was before.

All the stars that we can see in the sky are light years away from the Earth. Some of them probably went out a long time ago, but the light that they transmitted still reaches us.

So, if nothing can travel faster than light, what happens if we put a spotlight on top of a train?

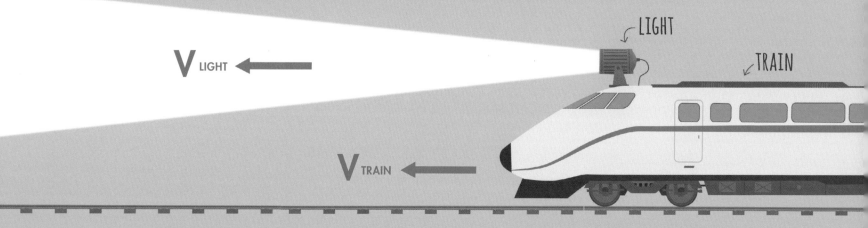

V LIGHT ←

LIGHT

TRAIN

V TRAIN ←

What speed is the light traveling at?

Just as Galileo told us, we should add the speed of the train to the speed of the light.

$$V_{LIGHT} + V_{TRAIN} = V_{LIGHT}$$

But as nothing goes faster than light, you cannot add (or subtract) speed to or from the speed of light.

!

We could put our spotlight on a snail, a racecar, or a space rocket, and **the light would always go at 300,000 kilometers per second.**

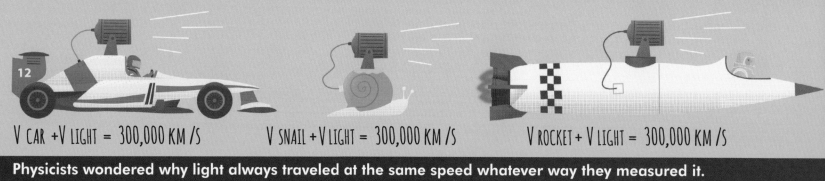

V CAR + V LIGHT = 300,000 KM /S   V SNAIL + V LIGHT = 300,000 KM /S   V ROCKET + V LIGHT = 300,000 KM /S

Physicists wondered why light always traveled at the same speed whatever way they measured it.
In 1905, Albert Einstein found an explanation.

Using only two ideas **1** if you go at a constant speed the laws of the Universe are always the same and **2** the speed of light is constant, however you measure it, Einstein created his famous theory:

THE **THEORY** of (Special) **RELATIVITY**

This theory has three incredible implications:

1 Time dilates

2 Length contracts

3 Mass increases

$\varepsilon = mc^2$

Einstein came up with two big theories, SPECIAL RELATIVITY, which is what we are looking at in this book, and GENERAL RELATIVITY, which is his theory about gravity.

TIME IS NOT WHAT IT SEEMS

One of the most surprising implications about light always traveling at the same speed is that time is not how we experience it in our daily lives.

Remember that even if we are sitting down reading a book, we are moving with our planet.

Time is an individual experience. Everybody has their 'own' time.

Time dilates according to the speed that we are moving: the faster we go, the slower time passes relative to someone who is at rest.

Time is not absolute

We have always thought that time is the same everywhere in the Universe. To put it another way, this precise moment on Earth is also happening on the Moon, Jupiter, Proxima Centauri, and on the far side of the Universe. Everyone, including great scientists like Galileo and Newton, all had this idea of time. The way we say it is that **TIME IS ABSOLUTE**.

Einstein was the first to realize that **TIME WAS SUSPECT** and that, in fact, it is not **ABSOLUTE** but it depends on which frame of reference we are measuring it from. In other words, **TIME IS RELATIVE**.

The speeds that we are capable of traveling with today's technology are too slow to notice the dilation of time.

The closer we get to the speed of light, the slower time passes.

Time dilates

One of the most fascinating consequences of this idea is that
TIME DOES NOT PASS AS QUICKLY WHEN WE ARE MOVING
AS WHEN WE ARE STATIONARY.

When Alice is traveling in the train and moving relative to Dr. Albert, time passes more slowly for her than for him. To put it another way, Alice's watch goes slower than Dr. Albert's, although the difference in the amount of time is so small that we don't notice it.

We say that time DILATES

To explain this idea better, we're going to do a series of thought experiments that will help us see clearly that time is not the same for everybody.

The faster Alice goes, the more time dilates and the slower her watch goes (for whoever sees her moving).

TIME DILATION

We're going to do a thought experiment.

1 – FIRING MARBLES

Below is a device or machine that fires marbles in opposite directions towards some detectors that have synchronized clocks, in other words, clocks that are showing the same time. When a marble hits a detector, the time that it took to get from the machine to the detector is recorded.

Alice and her machine are inside a train car that is traveling slowly and Dr. Albert is observing her from the platform on the station. Alice sets up the machine between two detectors inside the train, while Dr. Albert uses detectors that he has on the platform to record when the marbles reach Alice's detectors.

When the marbles are fired, which one will reach the detectors first?

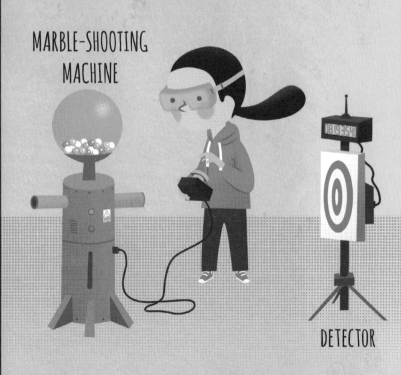

MARBLE-SHOOTING MACHINE

DETECTOR

A WHEN THE TRAIN IS STATIONARY

- We fire the marbles. The clocks show zero.

- The two marbles go at the same speed and are always the same distance from the detectors.

- Both Alice and Dr. Albert see the marbles reach the detectors at the same time. The clocks show the same time.

B WHEN THE TRAIN IS MOVING

- We fire the marbles. The clocks show zero.

- For Alice, the two marbles travel at the same speed.

- For Dr. Albert, the two marbles do **NOT** go at the same speed. The one that is traveling in the same direction as the train goes faster (adding up the speeds) and the one that is traveling in the opposite direction goes more slowly (subtracting the speeds).

- Both Alice and Dr. Albert see the marbles reach the detectors at the same time. The clocks show the same time.

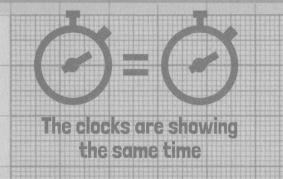

The clocks are showing the same time

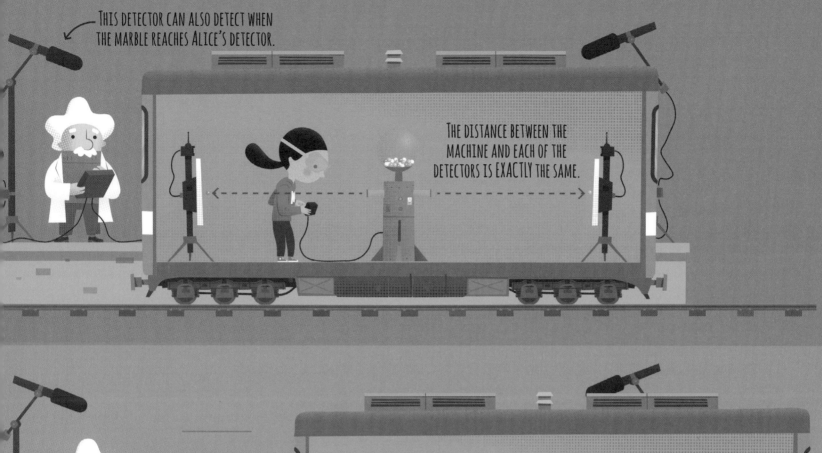

THIS DETECTOR CAN ALSO DETECT WHEN THE MARBLE REACHES ALICE'S DETECTOR.

THE DISTANCE BETWEEN THE MACHINE AND EACH OF THE DETECTORS IS EXACTLY THE SAME.

In the two experiments that we have done, the marbles reach the detectors simultaneously (at the same time) and both Alice's and Dr. Albert's clocks show the same time. So far, so good. The time is the same for everybody and nothing strange seems to be happening.

2 – FIRING PHOTONS (light)

Now we're going to do the same thing but, instead of marbles, we're going to fire photons (or light pulses) in opposite directions.

PHOTONS are particles of light that always travel at the speed of light wherever we are watching them from. In the case of photons, things **DON'T** happen as they do with marbles; Dr. Albert can't add or subtract the photons to or from the speed of the train.

THE SPEED OF LIGHT IS CONSTANT AND DOES NOT DEPEND ON THE FRAME OF REFERENCE

DETECTOR

PHOTON-SHOOTING MACHINE

A WHEN THE TRAIN IS STATIONARY

- We fire two photons. The clocks show zero.
- The photons go at the same speed and are always the same distance from the detectors.
- Both Alice and Dr. Albert see the photons reach the detectors at the same time. Both clocks show the same time.

← DETECTOR

PHOTON-SHOOTING MACHINE

B WHEN THE TRAIN IS MOVING

- We fire the photons. The clocks show zero.
- Alice sees the two photons traveling at the same speed and reaching the detectors at the same time.
- Dr. Albert also sees the photons going at the **SAME SPEED**, but in his case he sees the photon that is traveling in the opposite direction to the train reach the detector before the photon that is traveling in the same direction as the train.

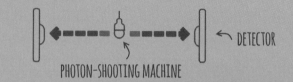

THIS IS HOW DR. ALBERT SEES IT.

The clocks are **NOT** showing the same time

WE HAVE CHANGED THE MARBLE-SHOOTING MACHINE FOR ONE THAT FIRES PHOTONS.

THIS IS WHERE IT STARTS TO GET STRANGE: for Alice, the photons arrive at the same time. For Dr. Albert, the one in front arrives after the one behind. How can the same event be seen in different ways? **THEY ARE DEFINITELY THE SAME PHOTONS!** Besides, when they look at the clocks, they realize that they are not synchronized any more: Alice's clock is slightly behind Dr. Albert's clock. **WHO IS RIGHT?**

Well, both of them are right. As we have already said, **TIME IS RELATIVE** and it is not the same for an observer who is moving as it is for one who is at rest. The faster Alice goes, the slower Dr. Albert will see time passing inside the train.

In order to check time dilation we're going to do a little experiment with a clock. But instead of using a normal clock with gears and hands, we're going to use one that is much simpler but also much more accurate:

A LIGHT CLOCK

To make a light clock, we place two different mirrors at a certain distance from one another, 1 meter for example, and we make a photon (light) bounce between them.

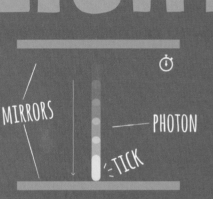

MIRRORS

PHOTON

TICK

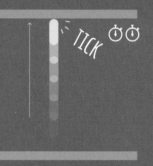

TICK

Distance = 1 meter

1 TICK = 1 meter

Every time that the photon bounces off a mirror we count a **TICK**. This is something that happens periodically, so we can use it to measure time. All we need to do is to count either how many **TICKS** there are or how many times the photon bounces off a mirror, which is the same thing.

As we know, the distance between the two mirrors is 1 meter so, for example, the photon covers **10 METERS** for every **10 TICKS**.

Now let's make things a bit more complicated. Dr. Albert stays on the ground with one light clock, while Alice boards a jet plane with another light clock.

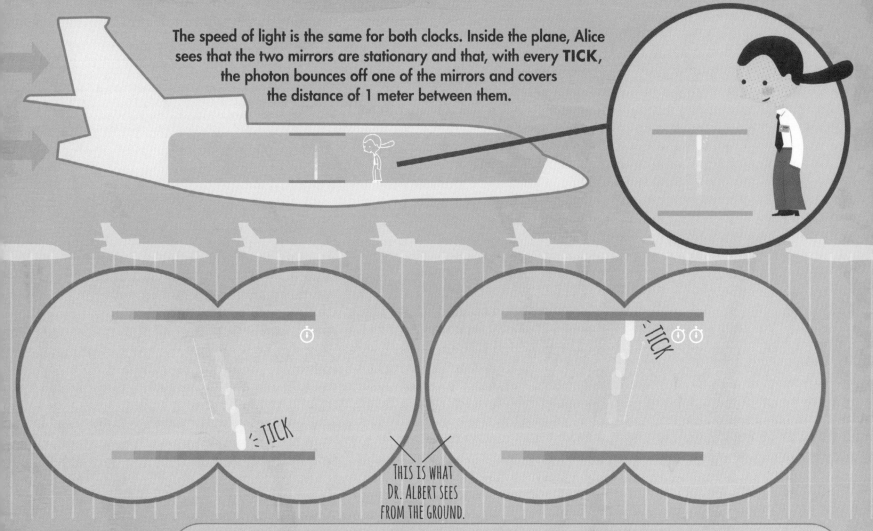

The speed of light is the same for both clocks. Inside the plane, Alice sees that the two mirrors are stationary and that, with every **TICK**, the photon bounces off one of the mirrors and covers the distance of 1 meter between them.

TICK

THIS IS WHAT
DR. ALBERT SEES
FROM THE GROUND.

Dr. Albert, who is stationary on the ground, also sees that his clock is stationary and that the photon covers 1 meter for every **TICK**.

But if Dr. Albert looks at Alice's clock inside the plane, he sees that the mirrors are **MOVING** and that the photon has to cover a distance of more than 1 meter. As the speed of the photon is always the same, it takes longer to get from one mirror to the other. Alice's clock is behind Dr. Albert's clock because her **TICK** takes longer to get from one mirror to the other. Time is different for Alice than it is for Dr. Albert, or **TIME HAS DILATED**, which is the same thing.

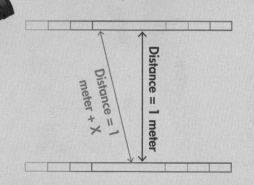

Distance = 1 meter

Distance = 1 meter + X

Distance = 1 meter

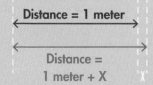

Distance = 1 meter

Distance = 1 meter + X

X

The two distances are different, but the photon still covers them in one **TICK**.

Strange, isn't it? So, what would happen to two friends of the same age if one of them traveled to another star at a speed close to the speed of light? Let's see >>

JOURNEY TO THE FUTURE

We already know that **TIME IS RELATIVE**; it doesn't pass as fast for observers who are moving (it goes more slowly for them) as it does for observers at rest.

This fact has been checked using two identical atomic clocks: one clock that we leave on the ground and another that we take up in a supersonic airplane that flies once around the planet. When the airplane lands, we notice that the clock that has been flying is several thousandths of a second behind the clock that is at rest.

The faster we go, the slower time passes.

So, since nothing can go faster than light, what would happen if someone went on a really, really long journey at a speed close to the speed of light?

Let's see >>>

Alice wants to travel to the nearest star to Earth. It is called **PROXIMA CENTAURI** and is 4.22 light years away. She says goodbye to her friend Bob, who is ten years old like her and will be waiting for her on Earth.

Bob is watching from Earth and confirms that the spaceship takes about 8½ years to do the return journey to Proxima Centauri.

When Alice steps down from the spaceship, she hardly recognizes Bob. He has become a grown-up man about to turn 19 while she is still a 10-year-old girl.

Because she traveled so fast in her spaceship, time for Alice has **DILATED**. Meanwhile, time on Earth has carried on the same as ever. What has been a few weeks' journey for Alice has been 8½ long years for Bob.

Traveling in a spaceship almost at the speed of light, it would take 4.22 years to go to Proxima Centauri and 4.22 to come back.

ALICE'S SPACESHIP

But because she is moving so fast, for Alice **TIME** passes much more slowly than on Earth. The outward journey takes more than four Earth years, while for Alice in the spaceship, only a few weeks go by.

PROXIMA CENTAURI IS PART OF THE ALPHA CENTAURI SYSTEM AND IS THE NEAREST STAR TO EARTH.

When Alice reaches the star, she turns around and heads back to Earth.

PROXIMA CENTAURI IS A KIND OF STAR CALLED A 'RED DWARF'.

TIME in the spaceship on the return journey continues passing very slowly as it did on the outward journey, and for Alice only a few weeks have gone by since she left Proxima Centauri. But on Earth, Bob once again confirms that the spaceship takes another 4.22 years to complete the return journey.

TRAVELING AT HIGH SPEEDS IS A WAY OF TRAVELING THROUGH TIME TOWARD THE FUTURE.

LENGTH CONTRACTION

One of the other fascinating consequences of **RELATIVITY** is that when we observe an object moving we can see it becoming more and more squashed as its speed increases.

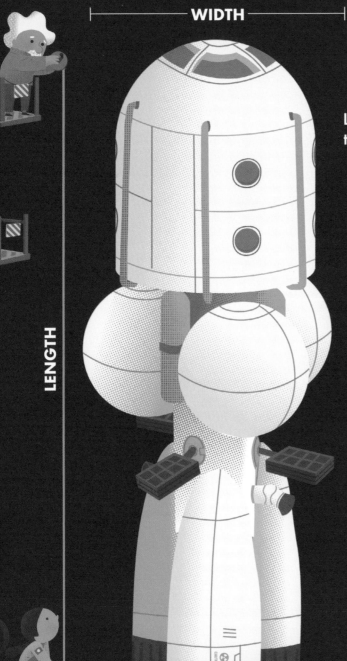

WIDTH

LENGTH

It shrinks in length!

Let's start with Alice and Dr. Albert measuring the length of their spaceship when it is stationary in the space station.

The spaceship then leaves for Proxima Centauri. As it accelerates towards the speed of light, Dr. Albert can see that the speed is affecting the length of the spaceship, making it shorter.

345.000.22

PROXIMA
CENTAURI

When the spaceship has only just left and is still moving at low speeds, it is more or less the same length as when they measured it in the space station.

As the spaceship accelerates and approaches the speed of light, Dr. Albert sees that it is contracting in length but Alice, who is traveling inside, doesn't notice any changes.

CAREFUL! The length only contracts in the direction of movement. The spaceship gets shorter lengthwise, but it is still the same width.

The muon's journey

There is an example in real life that we can use to check time dilation and length contraction. It is called a MUON.

Muons are formed when cosmic rays collide with air molecules in the upper layers of the atmosphere.

A MUON IS AN ELEMENTARY PARTICLE OF THE ELECTRON FAMILY THAT WEIGHS ABOUT 200 TIMES MORE THAN AN ELECTRON.

They have a very short life, as they only take 0.0000022 seconds to disintegrate.

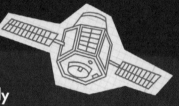

COSMIC RAY

During their short lives they can only cover 660 meters, traveling at almost the speed of light.

ATMOSPHERE

10 KILOMETERS

We can actually detect them in laboratories located on the Earth's surface, 10 kilometers below where they are formed.

MUON

MUON DETECTOR

But if they can only cover 660 meters, how do they travel 10 kilometers to detectors on the Earth's surface?

EARTH'S SURFACE

RELATIVITY gives us the answer to this puzzle

From the Earth:

We see that a muon travels very fast, almost at the speed of light. So we see that **THE MUON'S TIME DILATES** and becomes slower, which means that it takes 20 times longer to break apart. And as it takes longer to disintegrate, this means that it can cover a much bigger distance, far enough to be able to reach the Earth's surface where we can detect it.

TIME DILATION

Its life span is **0.0000022** seconds

Its life span is **0.000044** seconds

From the muon's point of view:

It also sees the Earth approaching very fast, almost at the speed of light, so it sees **DISTANCES GETTING SHORTER (LENGTH CONTRACTION)** and the **EARTH'S SURFACE, INSTEAD OF BEING 10 KILOMETERS AWAY, IS ONLY ABOUT 500 METERS AWAY**, which gives the muon time to reach the ground before disintegrating.

LENGTH CONTRACTION

The distance between the place where it is formed and the Earth's surface is about 500 meters.

The distance between the place where it is formed and the Earth's surface is 10 kilometers.

The muon has more time to travel from the Earth's point of view, and less distance to cover from its own point of view. This is why we can detect it in our laboratories.

SPEED MAKES THINGS HEAVIER

Another surprising consequence of **RELATIVITY** is that **AS THE SPEED OF AN OBJECT INCREASES, SO DOES ITS MASS!**

ENGINES PROVIDE THE ENERGY NEEDED FOR THE SPACESHIP TO MOVE.

THE ENERGY NEEDED

When we weigh ourselves on the scale at home, we are weighing our **REST MASS. REST MASS** is the mass of an object when it is stationary.

The more mass a body has, the more energy is needed to push it and make it move.

In Alice's interstellar journey, we saw her spaceship approach the speed of light.

Watching from Earth, we can check that as the speed of the spaceship increases it becomes harder to make it accelerate. In other words, more energy is needed to push it because the mass of the spaceship increases as it approaches the speed of light.

There comes a point when the spaceship has so much mass that it is impossible to carry on pushing it.

$$E = mc^2$$

This is why an object with mass **CANNOT** go at the speed of light because as it accelerates, the mass grows and grows until it becomes **ENORMOUS**.

If we reached the speed of light, the mass would become **INFINITE** and we would have to use lots and lots of energy, more than all the energy that exists in the Universe. We would need **INFINITE** energy.

Remember: nothing can go faster than the speed of light.

PHOTONS, or light particles, have something very unusual and strange about them: THEY DON'T HAVE ANY MASS. To put it a better way, when they move, they always move at the speed of light; they are never stationary. This means that we can't measure their REST MASS.

Surfing the LIGHT

When he was very young (just 16 years old), Einstein wondered what it would be like to travel on a beam of light.

This was one of Einstein's first thought experiments.

PHOTO OF ALBERT EINSTEIN AT THE AGE OF 14

Einstein imagined that riding a beam of light would be cool and fun, but there was something that he wasn't sure about: what would another beam of light look like if it was traveling beside him at the same speed?

At first he thought that it would appear stationary, not moving, at zero velocity relative to him, just like when we see a car traveling at the same speed as our car on a motorway. But then Einstein realized that this would be very strange. No one had ever seen a stationary beam of light.

No one could give him an answer to this question, so he carried on mulling it over to try and find a solution. It took him ten years to solve the puzzle. He was 26 years old when he worked out the **SPECIAL THEORY OF RELATIVITY,** which, as we know, says that light always travels at the same speed, however you look at it.

Young Einstein's answer to the puzzle was that if you were traveling on a beam of light, you would never see another beam of light staying still. You would always see it traveling relative to yourself at 300,000 km/s, the speed of light.

What's more, however hard you try, you are never moving relative to yourself. You are always at rest relative to yourself, whether you are in your living room at home, in a train car, or flying in a plane.

This means that the TICK-TOCK of your watch will always take the same amount of time. In other words, your own time will not dilate.

When you measure yourself, your height and width do not change (they do not contract) and every time you stand on your scales, your mass never varies (it does not increase).*

*As long as you haven't grown in the meantime, of course!

REMEMBER
Time dilates, length contracts, and mass increases whenever we observe objects moving relative to ourselves. This is what Einstein calls his theory of **RELATIVITY**.

A Mathematical Universe

Einstein apparently took ten years to understand the ideas in his theory of special **RELATIVITY** and just a few weeks to find the mathematical equations that describe it. Here are some of these equations so that you can see how cool they are:

The Lorentz transformations

$$ct' = \gamma(ct - \beta x)$$
$$x' = \gamma(x - \beta ct)$$
$$y' = y$$
$$z' = z$$

The Lorentz factor

$$\gamma = \frac{1}{\sqrt{1 - \dfrac{v^2}{c^2}}} \qquad \beta = \frac{v}{c}$$

Mass-energy equivalence

One of the most famous equations in the world.

$$E = mc^2$$

REST MASS

$$m = m_0\,\gamma$$

Photon energy

This is the energy of a light particle (otherwise known as a photon).

$$E = h\nu$$

Speed of light:
(in a vacuum)

$$c = 299{,}792{,}458 \text{ m/s}$$

ACKNOWLEDGEMENTS

Sheddad To my two main physicists, **Carles Muñoz** and **Diego Jurado**, for improving this book with their wise comments.

To my friend **Salva Sanchis** for his vision. To my darling **Helena** for proofreading and correcting the text and most of all for always being there. To **Unai** and **Tarek** for the chats about physics in the car that have helped me so much with this book. And to Inma, as always. Thanks to them, it all makes sense.

Eduard Many thanks to all the people who have made this book possible, especially **Meli**, but also **Pere**, **Lourdes**, and **Ariadna**, for their constant support and infinite patience.

And to all the scientists, both men and women, whose work has made, is making, and will continue to make it possible to go further and further.

Button Books